THE
PANIC
BUTTON
BOOK

This book is dedicated to all the kids with worries on their mind – the big thinkers, the creative beings, the switched-on kids, the sensitive souls, the nurturers, the frustrated inventors and those who see the world in a different way. From my heart to yours, I'm sending you calm, deep breaths and a lightness to layer into your days.

•

For all the mums, dads and caregivers of these sensitive, brave souls, you've got this. Even on the tantrummy days, the teary mornings, the upset evenings, you've got this. Your little somebody selected you as the best possible person to help guide and nurture them through their lives and that means something.

THE
PANIC
BUTTON
BOOK

FOR
KIDS

An interactive guide
to help kids deal with
worries and feel calmer

TAMMI KIRKNESS

murdoch books
Sydney | London

Contents

Tammi's story **4**
Note to parents & caregivers **5**
Helpful tips for parents & caregivers **6**
How to use this book **8**

PART ONE

HOW DO I FEEL? 11

•

PART TWO

FEELING MY FEELINGS 17

•

PART THREE

**FIGURING OUT WHERE THE
WORRY STARTED 43**

School **46**
The people in my life **66**
Home & family **94**
Something else **104**

•

PART FOUR

CHECKING IN AGAIN 129

Helpful calming rituals for your child **136**
Affirmations **138**
The Anytime Meditation Script **140**

Acknowledgements **142**
Resources **143**

Tammi's story

•

When I was a kid I tried really hard to make no mistakes. I often compared myself to other kids I knew. I left my homework to the last minute and I was really hard on myself if I didn't do something perfectly. Overall, I was a bit of a worrier.

When I grew up I realised that other kids and adults sometimes worried as much as I did, and that was a huge relief. To try to learn more about how our minds work, I read everything I could about why this happens to some, but not so much to others. I studied psychology and worked as a clinician in a London-based centre for kids with learning difficulties, which often went hand in hand with having a little worried mind. In the south of India I trained with monks to become a yoga teacher, I've run a busy coaching practice in Sydney, and also work as a meditation instructor, Clinical EFT Practitioner and anxiety specialist.

I wrote this book to help encourage a common language for parents and their kids who worry a lot, and to help teach kids ways to cope. Remember, kids are incredible. The more we empower them to acknowledge their feelings and provide a safe space to process them, the happier they are.

NOTE TO PARENTS & CAREGIVERS

Anxiety can affect anyone of any age. It's tempting to want to protect kids from things that make them worry. However, we know that the more we can help them feel their fears and still do the things they want and need to, the more resilient they will be. When we can talk about fear and worry with kids, it can help to destigmatise and normalise the feelings.

The messages in this book draw on yoga and breathing techniques, psychological approaches, emotional freedom techniques (EFT), life coaching practices, clinical processes and my own experiences as a young overthinker. We don't choose whether or not to be anxious, but we can choose how to manage the feeling when it arises. Working through these feelings and sensations can help us to grow, build flexibility and foster courage. If at any point your child needs individualised support, please reach out to a relevant qualified support partner, such as a counsellor, psychologist or therapist.

Helping someone through emotionally sticky times can act as a mirror to how you cope with that issue, too. As you work through this book and the emotional management journey with your young person, it may bring some of your own anxieties to the surface. If this happens, that's okay. It's an opportunity for you to heal and process things that may have been buried for a while. The more you learn to manage your own mental wellbeing, the more you will have in your toolkit to be a safe place to land for others. Remember, the most beautiful people are those who are unique and on their own learning journey.

HELPFUL

TIPS

for parents
& caregivers

Model upbeat, confident thinking.

Remember that you don't need to be perfect to help your child.

Take care of your own emotional wellbeing.

Balance both learning and play.

Give your child the space to make mistakes by not completing their homework on their behalf.

Do your best to not get emotionally swept up in your child's feelings.

Remember that all feelings are acceptable, but all behaviour is not. Do your best to manage unhelpful behaviours while ensuring family boundaries are upheld.

Focus on your child's efforts, not their outcomes.

When appropriate, share your own examples of making errors or times when you've felt nervous and how you got through them.

Aim to have a light and centred approach when talking about feelings.

If your child's anxiety continues, or could be the result of a traumatic experience, reach out for professional help.

How to use this book

•

This book is split into four parts. The first, 'How do I feel?', is where you'll start each time. The second, 'Feeling my feelings', covers the most common anxiety-based symptoms and feelings. The third part, 'Figuring out where the worry started', dives deeper into triggers or anxiety-inducing areas. The last part lets you check in again on how your child is feeling. Simply follow the prompts to the relevant section.

This book is full of interactive questions for you to read with, or to, your child, depending on their age. As you read, gently encourage your child to respond. When there are activity prompts, such as deep breathing, I encourage you to do these along with your child. Whenever possible, in between readings of the book, say positive things to your child about the effort they make each time they use these techniques.

On many pages you'll find notes to parents and caregivers – these are to help you understand the context behind particular questions and why certain techniques are being used. Depending on your child's age, you may or may not choose to read these out loud. When activities prompt kids to repeat something out loud, break it up into short chunks so they can easily repeat it back.

If your child shows signs of feeling better, such as having a brighter face, looser body language, slowed breathing or other signs of relaxing, ask them if they are feeling better. If they are, ask them if they would like to finish the book there and if they would, gently turn to page 135 and read it out before finishing up.

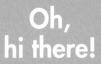

Oh, hi there!

Let's get started ...

Sometimes it's tricky being a kid. There are so many things to learn and new feelings seem to keep popping up. Sometimes other kids' lives look as if they're easier than ours, and that can feel upsetting.

When big feelings come up, they can be hard to deal with, and when we are worrying on our own we can feel lonely and scared.

When we worry, it's as if we give away some of our happiness. It can help if we understand why it is happening, because then we can do something about it.

You are a beautiful, clever kid and it's important you remember that.

To try to understand all of the things going on in your mind, we're going to follow the arrows.

Your friend, Tammi

PART ONE

How do I feel?

Feelings are beautiful things.
They send us messages about how
we're reacting to the world around us.
To get started, let's check how
you're feeling right now.

Right now,
WHICH FACE
describes how
you are
FEELING?

WE'LL CHECK IN WITH THESE
AGAIN AT THE END.

SAD

ANGRY

SILLY

HAPPY

FRUSTRATED

SHY

SCARED

EXCITED

WORRIED

LONELY

LEFT OUT

OVERWHELMED

TIRED

SICK

EMBARRASSED

CALM

*NOTE TO PARENTS: *Being able to identify which emotion is present can sometimes bring instant relief to an overwhelmed individual.*

On a scale from 1 to 10, how **STRONG** are those **FEELINGS?**

*NOTE TO PARENTS: By understanding the intensity of the worry, it allows for clearer understanding between parent and child of the current moment's severity. Additionally, tracking it (we will check in with this scale at the end of the book), can give clues about what brings relief.

15

PART TWO

Feeling my feelings

Sometimes we feel great and sometimes not so great, but all feelings are important. The more we understand them, the easier things are to cope with. Now we're going to check in with the most common parts of worry.

Do you have any of these things happening right now?

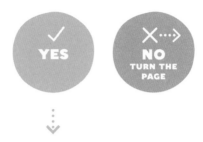

Think about that area
of your body.

Take a big breath
into that area.

With a big breath out,
breathe out the worry.

Repeat twice more.

*NOTE TO PARENTS: *Deep breaths bring extra oxygen
to the brain, allowing the body to relax. Physical sensations are like
messengers – they are there to tell us something is going on that might
need our attention, or that we've surpassed our processing capacity.*

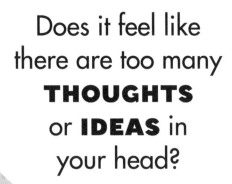

Does it feel like there are too many **THOUGHTS** or **IDEAS** in your head?

Stand up.

Bend over like you're going
to touch your toes.

Hold on to each elbow and
dangle forward like a rag doll.

Picture all of the unhelpful
thoughts falling out of the top
of your head.

After about 20 seconds,
gently stand back up.

Wiggle one of your fingers.

Wiggle a second finger.

Try to wiggle your nose.

Shrug your shoulders.

Shake one leg.

Shake your other leg.

Are you up for the big shaking finale?

Stand up and shake your whole body out!

*NOTE TO PARENTS: *When we feel anxious our body often tenses up. Because our mind and body are so closely linked, when we physically shake our body out, it can act as a quick, in-the-moment reset.*

Are you **THINKING** about something **OVER** and **OVER** again?

YES

NO
TURN THE PAGE

We're going to have a
really good go at worrying.

Have Mum or Dad,
or another grown-up, set a timer
for three minutes. During this time
you can worry as much as possible.
When the timer finishes, it's
time to stop worrying.

Before you start, choose from one of these ways to get all your worries out. You can:

List them out loud

Whisper them into your toy's ear

Write them down

Draw them in a picture

Now, start the timer and start worrying.

After the timer ends, take a big breath in and then a big breath out.

....

....

....

....

....

....

....

....

....

BONUS: *It's not essential, but if you think it might help, you and your child could brainstorm some potential solutions to the worries that they listed.*

Do you still feel
STUCK? Like you
want to **YELL?**
Or that you want
to **RUN** away?

It sounds like you've just had a big shock.
When something frightens us, we often act just like animals do.

When animals are scared, they either freeze completely still,
or get ready to fight or run away quickly.

To help your body return to a feeling of safety, go and get
a cup of water.

Pour a mouthful of water into your mouth and gargle it.
(If you can't gargle, or you don't have any water, just take
a breath in through your nose and out through your mouth and
then sing a short song, such as 'Happy Birthday'.)

*NOTE TO PARENTS: *Gargling and singing both stimulate the vagus nerve
(the body's largest cranial nerve), helping to regulate the parasympathetic
nervous system, which is responsible for initiating a feeling of calm.*

Is something
making you feel
NERVOUS?

Close your eyes (if that feels okay).

Imagine your nervousness is a shape floating
in the air in front of you.

What colour is it?

What shape is it?

What texture is it?

Notice how it's outside of you. By using big breaths,
blow this shape away and up into the sky.

Shrug your shoulders and feel a sense of release.

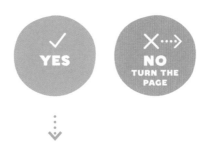

Switch off all gadgets including phones, tablets, games, computers and the TV. Turn off or dim all overhead lights.

Is it bedtime?

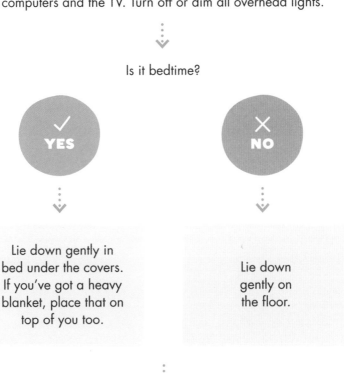

Lie down gently in bed under the covers. If you've got a heavy blanket, place that on top of you too.

Lie down gently on the floor.

Place your hands on your belly. As you slowly breathe in and out, notice how your belly goes up and down under your hands. Do this five times.

Have you been **MEAN** to yourself?

Just as it's important to be kind to our friends, it's important to be kind to ourselves.

Let's remember some of the wonderful things about you.

List three things you like about yourself. For example, you have a clever brain, are a good friend and can tell funny jokes.

Repeat out loud,
'I choose to speak kindly to myself for the rest of the day.'

Breathe in deeply. Breathe out all meanness.

Do your best to sit
or stand still.

Close your eyes.

Picture long tree roots coming out
of your feet down into the earth.

Imagine how peaceful it is
down there.

Breathe up some of that peace into
your feet and body.

Open your eyes.

Are you
feeling
FIDGETY?

YES

NO
TURN THE PAGE

Lie on your back
and place a closed
book on your tummy.

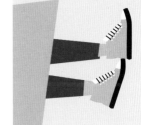

As you breathe in,
notice how the
book rises.

As you breathe out,
notice how the
book lowers.

Do this five times.

Gently stand up.

Can you roll your tongue?

Roll your tongue.

Breathe in and out three times.

Do you notice that the air seems cooler as you breathe it in this way?

Pretend you are a fan and gently blow air on your left arm, moving your head side to side as you do it.

Now gently blow air on your right arm in the same way.

*NOTE TO PARENTS: *This is a breathing technique from the yogic tradition to help cool someone down, both physically and emotionally. Roughly three to four out of five people can roll their tongue – if it doesn't come naturally to your child, don't force it (see Resources, page 143).*

PART THREE

Figuring out where the worry started

When we understand where our worry started, it can often help. Let's try figuring it out.

Are you feeling **WORRIED** about …

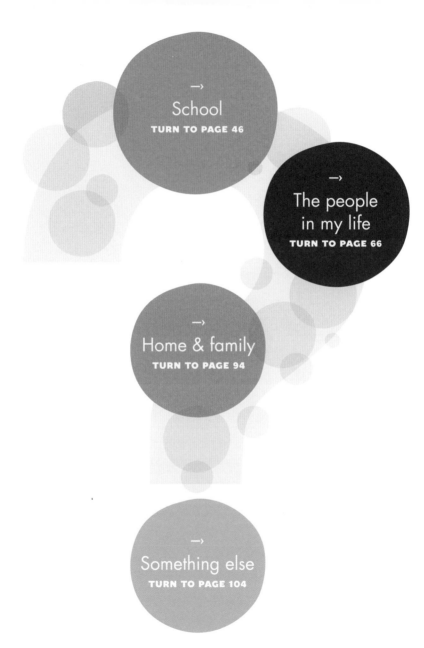

→
School
TURN TO PAGE 46

→
The people
in my life
TURN TO PAGE 66

→
Home & family
TURN TO PAGE 94

→
Something else
TURN TO PAGE 104

*NOTE TO PARENTS: *If there are multiple areas causing the worry, prompt your child to pick the one that feels the strongest and start there.*

School

Coping in the schoolyard and classroom can be tricky. If you're feeling worried about something to do with school ...

TURN THE PAGE →

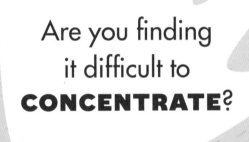

Are you finding
it difficult to
CONCENTRATE?

Bring your thoughts to the present moment
by finishing these sentences:

Right now, I can see …

I can hear …

I can smell …

I can taste …

I can feel …

*NOTE TO PARENTS: *This tool of 'mindfulness', used to bring attention
into the present moment, makes it far easier to concentrate.*

Have you
done something
OVER and **OVER**
again, trying to
make it **PERFECT**?

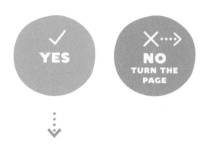

Remember, no matter what you create,
you are still a great kid.

If you mess something up and it doesn't look like
what you wanted it to, everything will be okay.

Take a guess now how long it might take you to
finish your task, such as until lunch or dinnertime.

Work on your task until that time rolls around,
then wherever you're up to is where you stop.

Remember, finishing something is better than having
something half done because you spent too long
trying to make it perfect.

*NOTE TO PARENTS: *When we try to make things perfect it leads us
into the trap of black-and-white thinking. When we think things are either
all good or all bad it loads the pressure on. Having the mindset that
someone is strong or weak, or smart or dumb, leaves little space to be
calm because we're all a mix of different qualities.*

Are you **LEAVING** something to the **LAST MINUTE**?

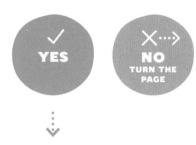

Say out loud what the thing is that you need to do.

Say out loud when you need to do it by.

Say out loud all the reasons you've been putting it off.

Come up with a way to deal with each of those reasons.

Can you do the thing right now?

Start it straight away.

Choose a time when you can start it and ask someone to remind you to begin it then.

Do you
need **HELP**
with something?

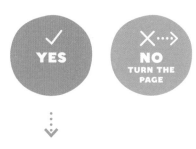

Say out loud what you need help with.

Think about who might have the skills to help you with this.

Do you know this person?

Go and ask them
for help.

Imagine what ideas this
person would have.

EXTRA NOTE: *Remember that asking for help shows bravery and strength.*

Have you **GIVEN UP** on something before really trying?

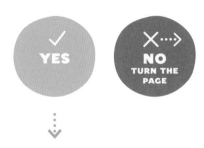

Say out loud the activity you are avoiding. For example, you might need to write a story for school.

Let's break down the task into smaller steps.

Get out a piece of paper.

Together with your parent or grown-up, write down all the steps you need to take to finish this task. With the story example, you might write down that you need to come up with a title, write the first sentence, write five more sentences, read it back to yourself, then hand it in to your teacher.

Put the steps in number order.

Decide when you will start step number 1.

*NOTE TO PARENTS: *Kids will often say an activity is 'boring' if they feel overwhelmed or out of their depth. If you hear this, ask which bit is the trickiest for them and if they'd like some help.*

Have you been **FOCUSING ON** the **PROBLEMS** with something you created or made?

Remember, there is no one 'right' way of doing things.

List out loud three things that you enjoyed while you were working on this.

List one thing that you like about your creation.

Breathe in deeply. Breathe out all feelings of trying to be perfect.

*NOTE TO PARENTS: *Emphasising the enjoyment of the creative process is vital to releasing the black-and-white thinking behind perfectionism.*

Does it feel as if something is **SO BAD** that it's like the end of the **WORLD**?

That can't feel nice.
Take a big breath in and a big breath out.

Say out loud what feels like the end of the world. For example,
'If I don't get a good grade, I'll be a terrible student.'

Does that thought feel helpful?

Out of 10 (10 being highest), how likely is that thought to be true?

Let's try looking at that thought another way. For example,
'This is just one of many tests, and my teacher has told me
she loves having me in her class as her student.'

Being able to think differently from others is a great gift, even if it doesn't always feel like that.

What are some of the good things that make your brain different? List two or three. For example, you can play music, draw cartoons or imagine different worlds.

Say out loud, '*I love my mind and my mind loves me. I choose to take care of it and be proud of how it works.*'

YES

NO
TURN TO PAGE 129

Choose which part of your life is still
on your mind from the below:

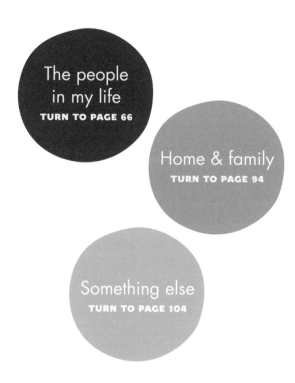

The people
in my life
TURN TO PAGE 66

Home & family
TURN TO PAGE 94

Something else
TURN TO PAGE 104

The
people in
my life

While our friends and family are often our favourite people, sometimes how we feel about them can get wobbly. If you're feeling worried about the people you know …

TURN THE PAGE →

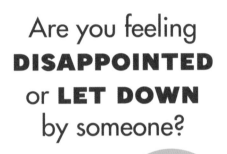

Are you feeling
DISAPPOINTED
or **LET DOWN**
by someone?

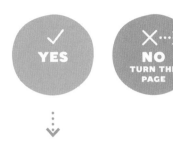

Is it fair to expect that person to have done
or said what you wanted?

If possible, go and
talk to this person
about your feelings.
If they aren't around
right now, choose a
time to talk to them.

Remember that
no one is perfect.
Notice where in
your body the
disappointed feeling
is, and then let it
float up and away.

Breathe in deeply. Breathe out all tightness
from your body.

Are you really sure that you have upset them?

It's time to say sorry. To get ready to give a really great apology, say these things out loud right now:

- What you did that was hurtful.

- A guess at how the person might be feeling.

- How you're going to stop it from happening again.

Go to the person and say sorry, mentioning all the things you just listed out loud.

Perhaps they aren't upset.

To double check, you can go and ask them if you hurt them. If they say yes …

Are you **PRETENDING** to like something to make someone else happy or to look **COOL**?

Would you still act this way or like this thing if no one else did?

Even though you enjoy acting this way, if it no longer makes you feel happy in the future, remember you can stop.

While it might feel easier to fit in if you like the things other people like, in the end it's best to be yourself. It's time to finish pretending and make more time for being yourself and enjoying the things you really like!

Breathe in deeply. Breathe out any pressure.

Keep being you and remember to always treasure your own opinions.

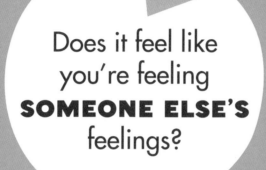

Does it feel like
you're feeling
SOMEONE ELSE'S
feelings?

Repeat out loud, '*Even though I care a lot about others, it's not my job to feel other people's feelings. I choose now to breathe out all feelings that aren't mine.*'

Take a big, deep breath in. Breathe out everyone else's worries and feelings.

*NOTE TO PARENTS: *Kids who are particularly empathic can automatically feel the feelings of others. Once this increased emotional sensitivity is acknowledged and managed, it can be a gift later in life. However, it can often cause emotional fatigue in the short term and is worth keeping an eye on.*

Does it
BOTHER YOU that
one of your friends or
brothers and sisters
might be **BETTER AT
SOMETHING**
than you?

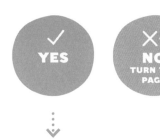

Everyone has their own talents and
it is very clever of you to see them
in someone else.

Say out loud one thing that you can learn
from the other person's talent.

Even if it feels tricky, take a moment
to think how happy you are that they
have such a great skill.

BONUS:
You could go
and tell them how
good they are at
that particular
thing.

Sometimes our brains feel like they freeze a little at the times when we want to speak. Say out loud what you wished you'd said at the time. Do you still want to say the thing to the person?

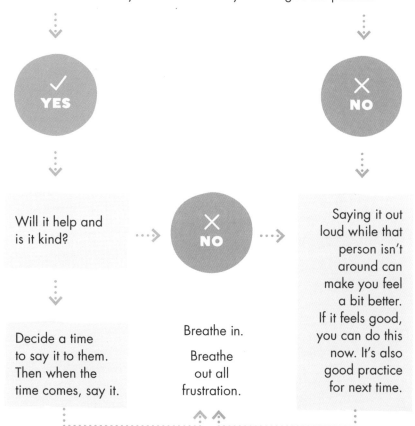

Will it help and is it kind?

Decide a time to say it to them. Then when the time comes, say it.

NO

Breathe in.

Breathe out all frustration.

NO

Saying it out loud while that person isn't around can make you feel a bit better. If it feels good, you can do this now. It's also good practice for next time.

Are you having a tricky time **MAKING NEW FRIENDS**?

YES

NO
TURN THE
PAGE

Let's figure out what's getting in the way of making new friends.

| Would some more confidence help? | Are you unsure where some nice kids might be? | Not sure how to say hello? | Don't know what to say after 'hello'? |

 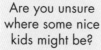

Stand up nice and tall and put your hands on your hips like Wonder Woman or Superman. Puff out your chest and look up to the sky.

Say out loud, '*I love being me. Other kids will enjoy being friends with me.*'

Think about your favourite hobbies such as playing soccer or chess.
↓
Find out where other kids are playing these games and go along and join in.
↓
When you find someone you like being around, ask them if they'd like to hang out with you on another day.

Turn to page 82 →

Have a question ready about something you're interested in.

For example, '*I played soccer on the weekend, what's your favourite sport?*' or '*I love dogs, what's your favourite animal?*'

Not sure **WHAT TO SAY** when you meet someone?

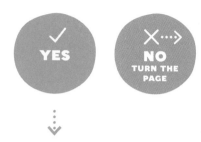

YES

NO
TURN THE
PAGE

The more you say hello to new people,
the easier it gets.

Let's have a practice with whoever
you're sitting with right now, but
pretend you don't know them.

Stand up straight.

Walk over to them.

Smile.

Say hello.

Ask a question. For example,
'What did you do on the weekend?'

Wait for them to answer.

In real life, this is when you would keep
on chatting, asking each other questions
and answering them, back and forth.

Are you
worried you'll
LOOK SILLY
doing something?

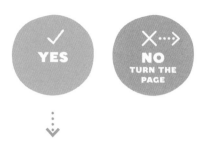

Let's switch out some of these pesky worries by swapping the nervous thoughts for confident ones.

Say out loud, *'Even though I might look silly doing*

_____

[insert thing above],

I'm still going to give it a go. And even if it doesn't work out, I will still be okay.'

Breathe in deeply. Breathe out all the nervous feelings.

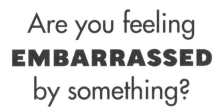

YES

NO
TURN THE
PAGE

Notice what embarrassment feels like
in your body. Maybe your face is red
or your hands are sweaty?

Pretend it's two weeks from now. You
are looking back on the thing that is
embarrassing you today. Are you okay?
What have you learnt?

Great job. Now say this out loud, '*I like
myself exactly as I am. I'm always doing
my best and it's okay to feel embarrassed.*'

Breathe in deeply. Breathe out
all embarrassment.

*NOTE TO PARENTS: *Embarrassment is the brain's reaction to
thinking we are being perceived in a way we don't like and
to feeling unacceptable in some way. It can be accompanied
by blushing, sweating, stammering and fidgeting.*

Is someone **BULLYING** or making fun of you?

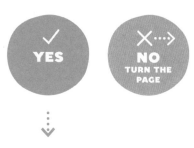

Remember, bullying is never okay.

Have you told someone or is something being done already?

Well done for speaking up. That was very brave of you. While you wait for something to be done, say out loud, *'I am brave and strong and I like myself exactly as I am.'*

It's time to tell someone what's happening.

As best as you can, explain what's been going on to a parent, teacher or another grown-up.

In the meantime, keep your distance from the bully, keep being kind to yourself and your friends, and remember how wonderful you are.

Is there an upcoming **ACTIVITY** that you don't want to do?

There are always going to be things we don't want to do, but part of growing up is having to do most of them anyway.

If you feel like you haven't practised or prepared enough, decide to do some more today.

In a friendly voice, repeat out loud, *'I've had plenty of practice, so I'm going to try my hardest and do my best to have fun.'*

Breathe in deeply. Breathe out all worry.

Are you
still feeling
WORRIED
about something?

YES ✓

NO ✗····>
TURN TO
PAGE 129

Choose which part of your life is still
on your mind from the below:

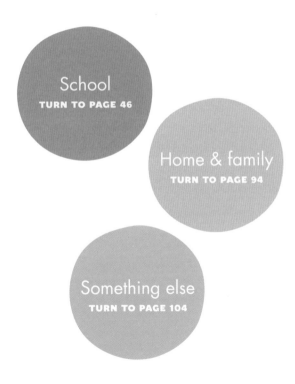

School
TURN TO PAGE 46

Home & family
TURN TO PAGE 94

Something else
TURN TO PAGE 104

Home
& family

Being at home with family is usually a place that we enjoy being, which feels safe. If you are feeling any worry about your home or family …

TURN THE PAGE →

Are you **FEELING SCARED** to leave your mum or dad to go somewhere or do something **ON YOUR OWN**?

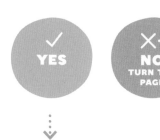

YES

NO
TURN THE
PAGE

The first few times we do something on our own it can feel scary. To help the unknown feel familiar, let's do some practising.

With one of your parents, pretend you're just about to say goodbye to them. Picture where you're standing (such as the school gates) and what you're wearing (such as your school uniform). Include a quick kiss, a special handshake or a wave. Once you've finished, say out loud one thing you liked about your practice and one thing that could help you feel more comfortable.

Next time you have to say goodbye, try to follow along with your practice.

*NOTE TO PARENTS: *The basis of separation anxiety isn't a behavioural problem to 'fix', it's an evolutionary instinct and a normal stage of childhood development. As such, it's best to avoid any urges to incentivise behaviour through rewards such as a treat to stop crying, even if it's tempting. If the anxiety is particularly intense or remains for an extended period of time, it might be time to connect with a professional.*

Are you being **GRUMPY** with your family?

Sit up nice and straight.

Close your eyes.

Put your hands over your heart.

Say out loud, *'May I be happy. May I be healthy. May I be peaceful.'*

Keep your eyes closed and picture your family in front of you.

Say out loud, *'May they be happy. May they be healthy.*
May they be peaceful.'

Open your eyes. Breathe in deeply. Breathe out all grumpiness.

*NOTE TO PARENTS: *This practice of 'loving kindness' helps*
to promote the feeling of peace and love within. It can also
diffuse frustration and emotional intensity.

Are you worried that something might **HAPPEN** to your **PARENTS**?

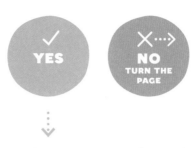

Everyone can get sick or injured at some point and it can be a scary thing to realise it might happen to your parents. Say out loud what you are frightened might happen. Is it likely that will happen?

Talk to your parents about your worries and ask how you might help them if the thing does happen.

Breathe in. Breathe out all worry.

Remember that even though scary things might happen in the world, it's nice to know this one isn't very common.

Breathe in. Breathe out all worry.

It's time now to do something fun. You could dance to some music, draw a picture, kick a ball around, or something else.

*NOTE TO PARENTS: *While these fears are real, after it's been talked through, distraction is key to ensure that the worry doesn't develop further.*

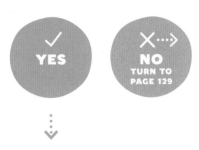

YES ✓

NO ✕···›
TURN TO PAGE 129

Choose which part of your life is still on
your mind from the below:

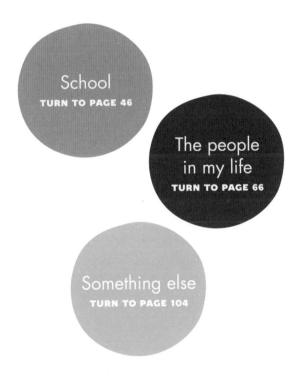

School
TURN TO PAGE 46

The people
in my life
TURN TO PAGE 66

Something else
TURN TO PAGE 104

Something else

Somedays we know exactly what is worrying us and other days not so much. Either way ...

TURN THE PAGE →

Big changes can feel both scary and exciting.

Fill in the blanks in the sentence below.

'Even though this big change feels

_____

[insert tricky emotions above],

one of the good things to come from it might be

_____ .

[insert good things above]

*For the rest of the day, I'm going to choose
to think about this good thing.'*

Breathe in. Breathe out all worry.

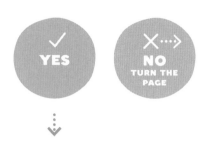

If you have a think about it, what's the reason you don't want to tell them?

You might get in trouble.	You might get someone else in trouble.	It's a bit embarrassing.
Keeping things to yourself can often make the problem seem bigger than it is. Remember that a problem shared is a problem halved.	While protecting others can be a good thing, often when we tell the truth it can feel like a big weight is lifted off our shoulders. Sometimes telling the truth can help protect others and keep them safe.	Remember that parents have also had all sorts of embarrassing moments of their own, and that they may be able to help, even if it's a bit uncomfortable to tell them something.

Decide whether you would now like to tell your parents.
If it's a yes, go and tell them now or sometime today.

Do you feel so **SAD** or **WORRIED** that your **HEART** hurts?

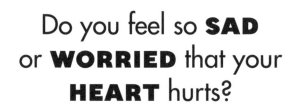

Ouch. To better understand how you're feeling, let's get drawing.

Get out a piece of paper.

Draw a picture of how your heart feels and what is happening inside of it.

Now that you can see your heart in front of you, say out loud what you think might help it to feel better. For example, it could be a hug or going outside for some fresh air.

If possible, go and do that thing.

*NOTE TO PARENTS: *Kids who are particularly emotionally sensitive often have extra awareness when it comes to other people's feelings and the emotional temperature of situations. Remember that this can be a helpful quality that, when nurtured, can allow kids to strengthen their intuition and creativity. Keep an eye out for any overstimulation that may exacerbate the more difficult parts of their sensitivity.*

EXTRA NOTE: *This might also be a nice time to do The Anytime Meditation Script on page 140.*

Have you seen something on **TV**, in a **BOOK** or on the **INTERNET** that has made you worried or scared?

Sometimes scary things happen and it's normal
to feel worried.

Say out loud what the scary thing is and how it's worried you.

Talk it through with a grown-up and ask any
questions you've got.

Breathe in deeply. Breathe out all worry.

*NOTE TO PARENTS: *If relevant, you could do the following:*

· On a map, show where the event happened to demonstrate
the big distance if it took place far away.

· Explain that replays on TV aren't the same event happening again.

· Talk about how rarely these events occur.

· Give facts that help debunk fears.

· Talk about who is helping in the situation, such as firefighters,
police or nurses.

· Where possible, limit media exposure to frightening topics.

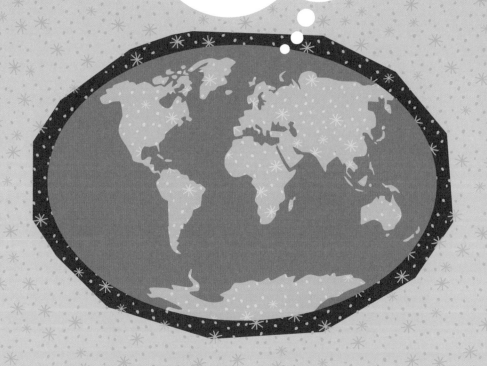

Big events can be scary for people of all ages.

Ask a grown-up any questions you've
got about it.

Now let's find some happy things going
on in the world.

Together with your parent, list two or more good
things happening in the world.

BONUS: Create a scrapbook of good things
happening in the world.

Does it feel like
you look **DIFFERENT**
from others?

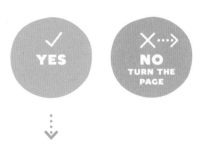

Did you know that every single body in the world is different? Identical twins even have differences! Even though it might be hard feeling like you look different, it's our differences that make us who we are.

List three amazing things your body can do.
Here are some ideas to get you started:

Run fast
Use a skipping rope
Catch a ball
See clearly
Hear when people speak
Smell chocolate
Climb a ladder
Make silly faces

Are you
struggling
to fall
ASLEEP?

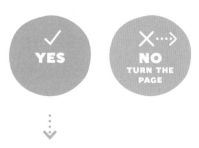

Sometimes our minds get very busy right before bedtime.
One of the reasons for this is that we may not have had enough
quiet time during the day. This means that when we finally
slow down, our brain bubbles over with too many thoughts.

To help find some calm, you can choose from one of these things to do:

Breathe.
Lie down in your
bed and take
three big deep
and slow breaths
in and out.

Read.
Choose one story
to read from your
bookshelf.

Meditate.
Ask a parent to read
out The Anytime
Meditation Script on
page 140 while you
lie down in bed with
your eyes closed.

*NOTE TO PARENTS: Remember people of all ages have trouble falling
asleep. If difficulty falling asleep is a common occurrence in your home,
you might like to consider how well the sleep hygiene (what happens in
the hours leading up to bedtime) is going. To improve it, in the hours before
bed consider ensuring no screens, no caffeine (remembering that chocolate
has caffeine in it), minimal sugar and no scary shows or stories, and try
dimming the lights and reading or playing calm music.*

Are you scared
of the **DARK**?

Say out loud what the scariest thing about the dark is for you.

Think of a way you could prove that worry to be untrue.

If that idea is possible right now, carry out your plan with
one of your parents or another grown-up.

For example, the scariest thing about the dark might be worry that
something is lurking in the shadows. An idea to prove that this isn't true
might be to shine a torch at the shadow and check there's nothing there.

DID YOU KNOW?
A very long time ago, when our ancestors lived outdoors
in nature and shared the land with possible enemies and
large animals, they learnt to be cautious of the dark. This fear
was helpful because it kept kids and babies from wandering
away in the middle of the night and helped keep everyone
safe. Now that we live in houses, that risk is something we
no longer have to worry about.

Are you
feeling
AFRAID
that there
is a **GHOST**
in the room?

Repeat this out loud,
*'I ask for all energy that is not mine to
please leave this room/house immediately.
Please leave peacefully and do not return.
I wish you well on your journey.'*

Picture that energy leaving.

Breathe in. Breathe out all feelings
of being scared.

---

*NOTE TO PARENTS: *The feeling of some other energy in the room can
be a very scary experience, particularly for kids. Whether their concerns
seem true or not, giving kids a voice in identifying what they feel
and being able to do something about it is very empowering.*

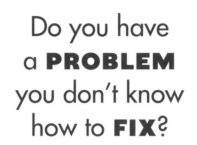

Do you have a **PROBLEM** you don't know how to **FIX**?

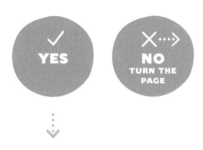

Do you feel comfortable saying your problem out loud?

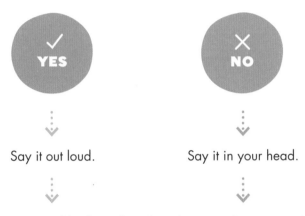

Say it out loud.

Say it in your head.

If a very wise owl had an idea about how to solve your problem, what do you think it might say?

Say out loud what first step you could take.

Do that first step.

Are you finding it **HARD** to **FIGURE OUT** what's making you feel worried?

YES

NO
TURN THE
PAGE

Tap on the 'karate chop' point of your hand.

Karate chop point

While you're tapping, say out loud three times,
*'Even though I don't know exactly what's making
me feel worried, I know I'm still a good kid.'*

While continuing to tap your hand, finally, say out loud
to yourself, *'Even though there might still be things on my mind,
I'm really proud of everything I've just worked through.'*

Stop tapping. Breathe in and breathe out.

*NOTE TO PARENTS: *This activity works best when you do it at the same time
as your child. It's recommended that you break up the statements into chunks
and your child repeats them after you. This technique is taken from the practice
of EFT (Emotional Freedom Techniques – see Resources on page 143).*

Checking in again

Let's check in with how
you're feeling now.

Right now, **WHICH FACE** describes how you are **FEELING?**

SAD ANGRY SILLY HAPPY

FRUSTRATED SHY SCARED EXCITED

WORRIED LONELY LEFT OUT OVERWHELMED

TIRED SICK EMBARRASSED CALM

*NOTE TO PARENTS: *Whether these feelings have shifted or stayed the same, remember that talking through them is always a good thing. Notice what did and didn't bring relief to your child. This will help inform your day-to-day emotional management and interactions.*

On a scale from 1 to 10, how **STRONG** are those **FEELINGS?**

1 ___ 2 ___ 3 ___

4 ___ 5 ___ 6 ___ 7 ___

8 ___ 9 ___ 10 ___

Did going through this book bring some calm?

YES

NO

How wonderful!

If there is anything else you know will help you feel better, it's time to mention it to your parent or grown-up to see if it can be done.

Well done for working your way
through all, or a little bit, of this book.
It takes lots of courage to talk about our
feelings and you have done exactly that.

Whenever you feel worried,
you can always read this book.

It's time to take a big breath in.
And a big breath out.

REMEMBER:
You have done a great job today.
You are very loved.
You are a great kid.

Helpful **CALMING** rituals for your child

To maintain momentum in between readings of this book, here are some extra activities you may like to try out with your child.

VISUALISATION
During bath or shower time, suggest that your child visualise all their worries washing off and going down the drain.

GRATITUDE
Before bed or at dinnertime, have everyone in your family say three things they are grateful for or enjoyed during their day.

GROUNDING

To help ground your child's energy, spend as much time as possible outside connecting with nature. This could include playing in parks, hiking, spending time at the beach or just having bare feet in your backyard.

MEDITATION

Instilling a meditation practice from a young age is a wonderful gift to your child. You might like to try some kids' meditations from an app or online, or read the one out on page 141. As a guide, kids can generally meditate for the number of minutes that correspond with their age, that is, a seven-year-old could work up to meditating for seven minutes.

EXERCISE

Make sure movement is part of your child's day, every day. Whether it's organised sports, playing on the nearest oval or walking the dog, it doesn't matter.

AFFIRMATIONS

Affirmations are a simple and effective way to help calm busy minds. They are positive statements that, when repeated, begin to feel and become true. You might like to read these out each morning with your child.

I am safe.

I am a good kid.

Trying my best is a great place to start.

I choose to feel peaceful.

I allow myself to have fun.

It's safe for me to breathe deeply.

My brain is amazing.

Interruptions are okay.

Mistakes help me learn.

I relax with every breath I take.

I am calm and comfortable.

The Anytime **MEDITATION** Script

Meditation is an amazing tool to help calm busy minds and hearts. It can give both kids and adults a sense of safety and peace that helps strengthen everyday resilience and happiness. Use the script opposite whenever your child needs it and enjoy the calm it brings you, too. It is recommended that you read this out calmly, slowly and with regular pauses to allow plenty of time for the visual components to be formed. It should take around three to five minutes.

To begin, have your child gently lie or sit down
with their eyes closed. Read out the following:

*As you settle in, start by taking a big breath in through your
nose, and now release that big breath out through your mouth.
I want you now to imagine high up in the sky above us the great,
big sun. Notice what shape the sun is and what colours it is made
up of. Now see a very large beam of sunshine coming down
from the sun all the way to your forehead. Feel the warmth of that
sunbeam as it dances on your face. Now let the warmth of the
sunshine start to fill up the whole of your head, helping it feel warm
and cosy. Watch as the warmth starts to move down your neck, your
arms and your chest. Notice how the warmth is now filling up your
belly, your legs and all the way down to your feet. Feel that
sunshine going into each toe.*

*I want you now to look into your body and notice if there are
any worries sitting inside. If you notice one or maybe even more,
know that you are safe. Now see the string of a balloon tying itself
to each of the worries. Notice what colour the balloons are and the
shape of the balloons. Now one by one, let each balloon float up
into the sky, taking your worries with them. As the worry leaves
your body, notice a feeling of lightness sweep through you.*

*Whenever you are ready, you can wiggle your toes.
Wiggle your fingers. Now gently blink your eyes back open.*

Acknowledgements

•

Creating books that make an impact is just one of the reasons I adore working with the team at Murdoch Books. Thank you to Jane Morrow for your capacity to see a whole book before the parts are crafted, to Virginia Birch for your editorial genius, to Britta Martins-Simon for sharing my books on a global scale, to Michelle Mackintosh and Kristy Allen for your creativity and design know-how, and to Sarah Hatton, Ariana Klepac and Lou Johnson; together you are game-changers, and you do it all with heart, intellect and grace.

In my experience, books are a culmination of experience, information, heart and the people who surround the author. For me to bring this book to life, a special thank-you goes to all the children and inner children who I've taught and coached. You remind me how to see the bright side of life and for that I'm grateful. To Taylan, Oakley, Kyla, Levi, Sydney and Madison, it's a joy to be a part of your family – thank you for continuing to teach me how to play. To Ivan, thank you for always being in my corner and for, together with me, bringing to the world our very own heart-filled human.

The biggest honour of my life has been becoming a mum to our Ruby. As you grow and learn, my wish is that you enjoy the full breadth of the world in all its complexity and that you treat your mind, body and spirit with kindness and awe. Thank you for choosing me to be your mum. You have brought me a calm and happiness that I have never before experienced.

P.S. For those who love the world's kids, a big thank-you for helping our next generation bolster their confidence, groundedness and self-respect. To the parents, teachers, childcare workers, psychologists, counsellors, grandparents, godparents, neighbours, health-care workers and playgroup leaders: by investing part of your energy into the kids of the world, you're making the earth a kinder, more productive, happier, better place. Thank you.

Resources

•

Page 41: bbc.com/future/article/20180130-do-you-inherit-the-ability-to-roll-your-tongue.

Page 127: The 'karate chop' technique forms part of Emotional Freedom Techniques (EFT) practice, developed by Gary Craig.

For emergency support, please contact your local helpline:

In Australia, this includes **Kids Helpline 1800 55 1800**

In the UK, this includes **ChildLine 0800 1111**

In the USA, this includes **Your Life Your Voice 1800 448 3000**

Published in 2021 by Murdoch Books, an imprint of Allen & Unwin

Murdoch Books Australia
83 Alexander Street Crows Nest NSW 2065 Phone: +61 (0)2 8425 0100
murdochbooks.com.au
info@murdochbooks.com.au

Murdoch Books UK
Ormond House
26–27 Boswell Street London WC1N 3JZ Phone: +44 (0) 20 8785 5995
murdochbooks.co.uk
info@murdochbooks.co.uk

For corporate orders and custom publishing, contact our business development team at
salesenquiries@murdochbooks.com.au

Publisher: Jane Morrow
Designer and Illustrator: Michelle Mackintosh
Design Manager: Kristy Allen
Editor: Ariana Klepac
Editorial Manager: Virginia Birch
Production Director: Lou Playfair

ISBN 978 1 92235 169 2 Australia
ISBN 978 1 91166 838 1 UK

 A catalogue record for this
book is available from the
National Library of Australia

A catalogue record for this book is available from the British Library
Printed by C & C Offset Printing Co. Ltd., China

**DISCLAIMER: The content presented in this book is meant for inspiration and informational
purposes only. The author and publisher claim no responsibility to any person or entity for
any liability, loss, or damage caused or alleged to be caused directly or indirectly as a result
of the use, application, or interpretation of the material in this book.**

10 9 8 7 6 5 4 3 2 1